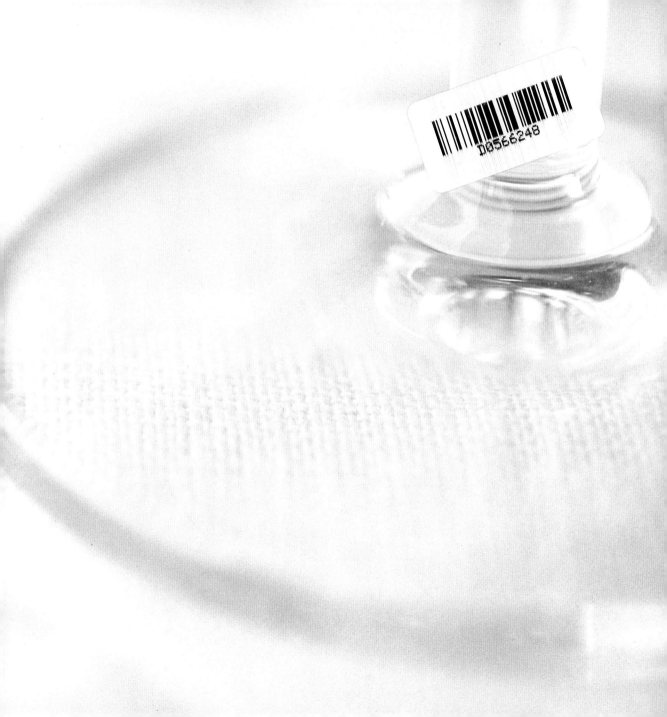

winetasting

winetasting

nicolle croft   photography by francesca yorke

RYLAND
PETERS
& SMALL
LONDON NEW YORK

To Alida who inspired me to start
my own journey into wine.

Senior Designer Susan Downing
Editor Miriam Hyslop
Production Deborah Wehner
Art Director Gabriella Le Grazie
Publishing Director Alison Starling

First published in Great Britain in 2002
by Ryland Peters & Small
Kirkman House
12–14 Whitfield Street
London W1T 2RP
www.rylandpeters.com

10 9 8 7 6 5 4 3 2 1

ISBN 1 84172 346 0

A CIP record for this book is available from the British
Library.

Printed in China.

contents

WHY WINE?   6

WHY ONE WINE TASTES
DIFFERENT FROM ANOTHER   8

SETTING UP A WINETASTING
AT HOME   14

THE ART OF TASTING WINE   22
Sight   24
Smell   30
Taste   34
Tasting Conclusions   45

TASTING NOTES TEMPLATE   46

KEY GRAPE VARIETIES   48

FOOD AND WINE MATCHING   56

WHITE AND ROSÉ WINE STYLES   58

RED WINE STYLES   60

GLOSSARY OF WINE WORDS   62

Index   63
Acknowledgments   64

why wine?

With more quality wine being produced and available at a wider price range than ever before, there has never been a better time to be interested in wine.

Its fascinating variety may make wine seem like a daunting subject to tackle. This book, however, focuses on the more general aspects of wine rather than the exceptions. It aims to unravel the world of wine, encouraging you, your friends and family to choose wines you may not have tried before, and to make the most of the amazing array of wine available.

At its most basic, wine is an agricultural product like cheese or bread. It is fermented grape juice made by turning the sugar in ripe grapes into alcohol. Yet it is a product with unique qualities that has captivated people and stimulated minds over thousands of years.

Wine can turn a simple meal into a special occasion. It is an excellent partner to food, whetting the appetite and aiding digestion. Wine can help to reduce cholesterol and provides an enjoyable source of vitamins and trace elements.

One of wine's greatest attributes is its complex variety. Wine can be made from hundreds of different grape varieties, in varying ways, all over the world. Wine is a living substance and evolves over time.

Appreciating wine is a unique experience for each individual. It depends on what you yourself do or do not like. As with art, you may prefer a particular style, Van Gogh to Mondrian for example. Have the confidence in your own taste which will undoubtedly change over time.

Wine can be appreciated on many levels. Getting to know wine is like getting to know a person. You can have friendly superficial contact or plumb intimate depths. One thing is for sure, with wine there is always another level to explore. You will never get to the point when you know everything. The deeper you go the better it becomes. This book will hopefully be the key to starting on this fascinating journey.

why one wine tastes different from another

Differences in taste in a wine are largely due to varying levels of 'acidity', 'sweetness', 'tannin' and 'alcohol'. These differences determine the type or 'style' of wine. We mainly use the 'body' and sweetness of a wine to divide wines into broad categories: fresh and dry whites, aromatic and medium-dry whites, 'rich' and full-bodied whites, sweet wines, rosé wines, light and fruity reds, smooth and medium-bodied reds and full-bodied reds.

Other variations of wine styles include 'fortified' wines, for example port or sherry which are strengthened with the addition of a spirit. 'Sparkling' wines are another style of wine. Most of these wines undergo a second 'fermentation' which produces bubbles.

But what gives each wine its individuality? This is due to the choice of grape variety, the region the wine was produced in, the year or 'vintage' it was made, the winemaker's input, and how old the wine is.

THE GRAPE VARIETY

Wines can be made from red or white grape varieties. The choice of which grapes to grow to make a wine is one of the most important factors in determining the taste of a wine. There are many to choose from. The producer's decision is mainly dictated by the soil and climate of the vineyard.

Grape varieties can be used individually to make wine. When only one grape variety is used, such as Chardonnay, it is called a 'varietal' wine. Wine is usually named after the grape variety in the newer wine producing countries in the world, such as Australia and California, as well as in the Alsace region of France and in Germany. Traditionally in Europe however, it is the region and not the grape variety that the wine is named after, as with Chablis in France for example (made from 100% Chardonnay).

Different grape varieties can also be 'blended'

or mixed together to make a wine. This is the case in Champagne where both red (Pinot Noir and Pinot Meunier) and white (Chardonnay) grape varieties are blended. Bordeaux is another region where varieties are blended together. Here it is the red varieties of Cabernet Sauvignon, Merlot and Cabernet Franc that are combined. This allows for greater 'complexity' as each grape variety adds its own individual characteristics to the wine.

Most grape varieties can be identified on the 'nose' and 'palate' by particular characteristics (see pages 48-55). These characteristics vary according to the climate where the grapes are grown. In hotter regions, for example, the flavours tend to be more intense and richer.

The age of the vine also affects the taste of wine. The older the vine, the fewer grapes are produced and the grape's flavours are more concentrated. Vines can grow to over one hundred years of age.

THE REGION

Grapes are grown for wine production within two bands around the world, between fifty and thirty degrees latitude north and south. It is within these bands that the climate is warm enough for the vine's grapes to ripen but cool enough for the grapes to maintain some acidity.

The wine producing areas in the northern hemisphere include North America and Europe, while in the southern hemisphere South America, South Africa, Australia and New Zealand produce wine.

In addition to geography, we also refer to wine regions in terms of when winemaking was introduced; the 'New' and 'Old World'. These are not exact definitions but used as an easy way to separate Europe (Old World) from newer wine producing countries. In the New World North America, South America, South Africa, Australia and New Zealand all produce wine.

Generally, cooler climates produce wines that have higher acidity and are more subtle in 'flavour'. Hotter climates produce wines with more fruit, alcohol and less acidity. This can be evident in the appearance, smell and taste of wines.

The area from which a wine originates has an effect on the wine's taste. This is due to differences in climate, soil and the 'lie of the land' or aspect. In Europe this is traditionally very important and referred to as 'terroir'.

The terroir forms the basis of different countries' classification systems; France's *Appellation Contrôlée* (AC), Spain's *Denominaciónes de Origén* (DO), Germany's *Qualitätswein bestimmter Anbaugebiete* (QbA) and *Qualitätswein mit Prädikat* (QmP) and Italy's *Denominazione*

Traditionally in Europe the wine is named after the region (left), yet in most newer wine producing countries wine is named after the grape variety (above).

di Origine Controllata (DOC). All of these classification systems impose a set of rules to try to ensure typicality of the *terroir*.

Choosing a wine with Appellation Contrôlée on the label guarantees that the wine has been produced within a designated wine producing region. It does not, unfortunately, guarantee quality. The only reliable guarantee of quality is the reputation of the producer.

In some Old World wine regions additional classification systems highlight vineyards which are seen as better than others. These are indicated on the wine label by such words as '*grand cru*' or '*premier cru*'. Be warned though, the level of quality indicated by these same words differs from region to region, and from producer to producer.

In the New World regions are stated on the label but there is no rigid system of classification. This gives producers greater freedom to experiment with different grape varieties and wine styles.

THE VINTAGE

The vintage of a wine refers to the year in which the grapes were harvested. Unless wines are blended from different years, the vintage is indicated on the label.

In cooler climates there is considerable variation between weather patterns from year to year. This has an effect on the characteristics of the wine produced. In hotter climates, there can be less variation from year to year and so the vintage is not such an important factor to consider when selecting wines.

the area
from which
a wine
originates
has an effect
on the wine's
taste

THE WINEMAKER

The winemaker can be compared to a chef. He or she may work to a standard recipe but will vary it according to the year and the grapes produced. When to pick to get perfectly ripe fruit, the temperature and length of fermentation, whether to use 'oak' and how long to mature the wine (if at all) and the timing of bottling are decisions that affect the taste and the quality of the wine.

Ageing wine in oak barrels before it is bottled gives the wine distinctive flavours. Using oak is like adding salt and pepper to your food. If done carefully it can enhance the flavours in a wine. If overdone it can mask the flavours.

Not all grape varieties cope with the oak's strong flavours, particularly white varieties.

AGEING

As wine is a living substance, its taste changes during its life-cycle. Most wines are made to be enjoyed young. They do not benefit from ageing and their life-cycles are short. A 'fine wine' is a general term for a wine made from superior quality grapes which warrants, for example, the investment of using oak barrels. These wines generally benefit from ageing in bottle and improve over time. When the wine's elements are in 'balance' the wine is ready to drink and tastes smooth.

White grape varieties that can age well include Chardonnay, Riesling, Chenin Blanc and Semillon. Red varieties that can improve with age include Cabernet Sauvignon, Merlot, Syrah/Shiraz, Nebbiolo, Sangiovese, Tempranillo and Pinot Noir.

setting up
a winetasting
at home

From left to right:
standard red wine
glass, traditional
Bordeaux glass,
standard white wine
glass, traditional
Burgundy glass,
standard tasting glass.

To taste wine in the comfort of your home all you need are your senses, a glass and some wine! It is worth following a few simple guidelines, however, to get the most out of the wines you are tasting.

WHAT YOU NEED
CORKSCREW AND FOIL-CUTTER OR KNIFE Make sure to cut the foil below the lip of the bottle of wine. TABLE WITH WHITE TABLE-CLOTH The white background helps to show up the colour of the wine. As an alternative a piece of white paper will do. TULIP-SHAPED GLASSES The best glasses for tasting are inward-curving to trap the wine's 'aromas' and direct them up to your nose, one of your most important tasting tools. Your glass should be made of clear, thin glass, and be stemmed to allow you to swirl and tilt the glass with-

out affecting the wine's temperature. Cupping the bowl in your hand will slowly warm the wine if necessary. GOOD LIGHT Daylight is ideal. NO SMOKE OR STRONG SMELLS NEUTRAL MOUTH Bread or plain water biscuits are excellent for cleansing the palate. WATER To sip during your tasting. SPITTOON A jug or funnel in a bottle will do. The decision to spit or not depends on the style of the tasting and how many wines you are trying. You do not need to swallow to taste the wine properly as most of your tastebuds are located on your tongue. Spitting out wine does help you to remain aware of each of the wine's individual flavours. Do remember though, a quantity of alcohol is still absorbed through the surface of the mouth even if you do spit.

HOW TO SET UP A TASTING

THE THEME Your tasting can be based on grape variety, region, or vintage for example, and can include both red and white wines. Do try to compare wines from a similar price bracket. It is a good idea to ask your guests to bring bottles that fit in with the theme. Try to do some research on the wines you are serving.

THE FORMAT This depends on how much space you have and if you want a formal or informal tasting.

FORMAL TASTING Using a glass for each wine enables you to compare the wines side-by-side in a formal tasting setting. Set out glasses on a table with a white table-cloth. Using tasting sheets enables each person to note their own views on each wine. It is simplest to photocopy the Tasting Notes sheet (page 46). If you are tasting several wines, provide a numbered sheet for each person on which to place the different glasses to avoid confusion. Do this by drawing around the base of the glasses on a sheet of paper and numbering the circles.

INFORMAL TASTING This can take place in your sitting room with guests sitting or standing, or at the dinner table throughout a meal. See page 56 for tips on food and wine matching. In a relaxed setting, using one glass for all the wines is adequate.

BLIND TASTING This involves removing all visual clues. Do this by wrapping the bottles in aluminium foil or brown paper to cover the label, or decant the wine into an empty bottle so that the bottle shape does not give

Different regions use different shaped bottles. From left to right: Bordeaux, German and Burgundy wines (above). For a blind tasting, it is a good idea to number the bottles to avoid confusion (right).

clues away. Label the covered bottles with numbers to avoid confusion. This enables you to rely solely on your senses for clues to the wine's identity. If you are a novice, blind tasting is an ideal way to learn the different flavours in wines without the distraction of labels.

THE NUMBER OF WINES Do not be tempted to taste too many wines. As a starter, taste two wines made from the same grape variety but from different parts of the world. Serve a maximum of six to eight wines.

HOW MUCH WINE IS NEEDED A tasting serving is only a third of a normal glass of wine. Each 75 cl bottle will give you approximately fifteen to twenty tasting servings. You can recork any wine that is left over.

OPEN AND TASTE Open the wines shortly before the tasting is due to begin and taste to check that the wines are in good 'condition'. Put the corks back in gently. See pages 30 and 32 for how to do this and which wine 'faults' to look out for.

DECANTING This involves pouring the wine out of the bottle into a decanter or jug. Decanting serves two purposes: removing sediment from a mature wine and 'softening' a firm young red wine. As it brings the wine into contact with the air it accelerates the wine's development. You can always swirl the wine around in your glass to achieve a similar effect. Allowing the wine to 'breathe' by simply leaving an opened bottle of wine to stand for an hour or two does virtually nothing towards 'aerating' and softening the wine.

TEMPERATURE Serving wine at the right temperature enables you to taste the wine at its full potential. If in

WINE SERVING TEMPERATURES

	REFRIGERATION	SERVING TEMPERATURE
WHITE WINES		
Sparkling	4 hours	5 – 10°c
Fresh and dry whites	1½ hours	10 – 12°c
Aromatic, medium-bodied dry whites	2 hours	10 – 12°c
Full-bodied sweet whites	1½ hours	10 – 12°c
Full-bodied dry whites	1 hour	12 – 16°c
ROSÉ WINES	1½ hours	10 – 12°c
RED WINES		
Light and fruity reds	1 hour	12 – 16°c
	STAND IN AN UNHEATED ROOM	**SERVING TEMPERATURE**
Medium-bodied reds	1 hour	14 – 17°c
Full-bodied reds	2 hours	15 – 18°c

doubt serve both red and white wines on the cooler side, particularly when tasting. Wines will, whatever the weather, warm up during the tasting. As chilling masks flavours, the more 'full-bodied' a wine the warmer it needs to be served. The 'tannin' level in a red wine is a guide to the temperature it should be served at. Red wines low in tannin can be lightly chilled. Forget 'room temperature', this expression was developed before the days of central heating.

SERVING ORDER This is fairly straightforward: dry before sweet, white before red, light before heavy, lesser before finer, young before old. This gives your tastebuds a chance to get used to the increasing strength or complexity, so that a wine is not over-shadowed by the one before it.

POUR THE WINES AND TASTE You can pour the wine, or you can pass the bottle around so those participating can look at the wine's label (unless tasting blind). Go through the tasting process together for each wine as guided by the Tasting Notes (page 46). Keep this book to hand to answer any questions that may arise.

PRESERVE ANY LEFT OVER WINES Wines do begin to deteriorate once opened. The more exposure to oxygen they have, the faster the wine 'oxidises', or goes off. Ultimately wine will turn to vinegar if left exposed to air. A bottle that is only half full will deteriorate faster than one that is nearly full. Removing the oxygen using a 'Vacuvin' pump or similar device means that the wine will stay 'fresh' longer. The higher the level of alcohol in the wine, the more resistant it is.

ice with
water in an
ice bucket
chills
better than
just ice

the art of
tasting wine

Each wine has a story to tell. Which grapes were used, where the grapes were grown, how the wine was made... The act of tasting wine, rather than simply drinking it, enables that story to be told through our senses of sight, smell and taste. As you look at, sniff and taste the wine, each sense confirms or rejects what the previous senses indicated. It is through this process that you are able to arrive at various conclusions about the wine.

This book explains how to read a wine's story; what to look out for, how to pick up on the information the wine is offering you and what that information can tell you.

You can enjoy music or art simply by listening or looking at it. A little added knowledge however, enhances your appreciation and understanding. Wine is the same. Simply drinking wine is without doubt a pleasurable experience. Learning more about wine will enable you to enjoy it even more.

The language of wine is often criticised for being verbose, exaggerated and meaningless. Do not let this intimidate you, try to describe what you are tasting with words that mean something to you.

Wine is unique in offering us a complex spectrum of flavours in a single mouthful. Its scope for complexity is unlike anything else we taste. We try to describe the flavours by comparing them with smells and tastes from our past experiences. Whenever I smell a mature wine from the Rhône Valley in France, I think of the leather seats of my father's old sports car. Words become triggers and can evoke special memories.

The flavours outlined on the following pages are only guidelines. They are not rigid, but ideas to get you started on preparing your own list of trigger words to describe wine. Remember it is down to your own individual perception and memories.

sight

Do not underestimate the importance of the eyes in the tasting process. Not only does sight give you clues about the wine's age and origin, it also helps you to decide whether the wine is in condition to taste at all.

WHAT TO DO

POUR THE WINE Use a simple inward-curving glass and fill to about a third full. This gives the wine room to move and 'breathe'.

HOLD THE GLASS BY THE STEM So as not to warm the wine and to allow you to see it easily, it is best to hold the stem of the glass, rather than the bowl.

TIP THE GLASS Tip at approximately 45 degrees against a white background to look at the wine's colour. Look at the centre of the wine (its 'core') and at its rim, or edge.

PLACE THE GLASS ON A WHITE SURFACE It is easiest to look at the 'intensity' or depth of the colour of the wine, by looking at it from above.

WHAT TO LOOK OUT FOR

CLARITY Does the wine look clear or dull? All wines should be clear and bright. If it is cloudy there is something wrong with it. As a back-up you could smell the wine to see if it smells unpleasant but a cloudy wine in itself is a reliable enough indicator of a faulty wine.

BUBBLES Is the wine fizzy or still? If it is not meant to have bubbles this may be a fault. Some wines however, which are meant to be drunk young, do have a 'spritz' or light sparkle.

TEXTURE Does the wine look oily or watery? Is it clinging to the sides of

Harmless tartrate crystals in a wine are a good sign as they show that the wine has not been over-treated.

the glass, known as 'legs'? This thickness or 'viscosity' indicates a high alcohol level and a concentration of ripe fruit, called 'extract'. In white wines it can also indicate sweetness.

DEPOSITS Can you see any deposit in the wine? This could be sediment from the ageing process which looks like sludge and is normally only found in red wines. This generally occurs in fine wines that have matured for several years.

You can also find crystals in either red or white wine which look like sugar granules. In red wines they are dyed red by the colour pigments. These are harmless and called 'tartrates'.

When opening a bottle if a few pieces of cork fall into the wine, just fish them out. They are harmless.

COLOUR The colour of a wine can give you an idea of what it is going to taste like. It can also indicate which type of grape it was made from, in which region the grapes were grown, what the weather was like during the growing season, and the wine's age.

As colour is affected by many factors, the following are general guidelines only.

The best way to describe colour is to compare it to things around you; the colour of your grandmother's plum jam or your mahogany dining room table. GRAPE VARIETY Certain grape varieties produce wines which are characteristically light or dark in colour. Sauvignon Blanc, Riesling and Chenin Blanc (when dry and young) produce light coloured white wines. Wines from Chardonnay, Viognier and Gewurztraminer (which often has a pinky tinge) are characteristically darker in colour. Pinot Noir and Grenache produce red wines which are light in colour and Cabernet Sauvignon, Zinfandel and Syrah produce darker coloured wines.

Colour in white wines comes mainly from the juice of the grapes, and ranges from pale lemon with green tinge to straw-yellow, and deep gold. White wines fermented and/or aged in oak can be a deeper gold.

Colour in red wines
comes from the contact
with the grape skins
during fermentation,
and ranges from purple
to crimson and red-brown.
Red wines have a large
spectrum of colours which
is useful in determining
grape variety and the
age of the wine.

Colour in rosé wines ranges from orange to pink. The colour in the best rosés comes from the skin of black grapes. The skins are left in contact with the fermenting grape juice for a short period.

REGION, CLIMATE AND THE WEATHER The cooler the climate, the lighter the colour of the wine. The hotter the climate, the riper the grapes, the thicker the skins and the darker the colour of the wines. White wines from the cold climates of Chablis in France or the Mosel in Germany can have a green tinge which comes from the chlorophyll in the scarcely ripe grapes.

AGE OF THE WINE Red and white wines become browner with age. This is caused by prolonged contact with air in the bottle which oxidises the wines. As they get older, red wines lose their youthful purple hues, and the red colour begins to break down. White wines darken with age, becoming golden brown.

STYLE OF THE WINE Generally the paler the colour, the lighter the wine's body, or the weight of the wine, in the mouth. With red wines, it is the intensity of the colour, rather than the colour itself which is the most useful indicator when looking at style.

DEPTH OF COLOUR Is the colour pale or intense? Is the colour uniform? If the colour of both red and white wines is intense it could indicate that the wines are full-bodied. The depth of colour in a red wine is a good indicator of age. An older wine is detectable by the 'breaking up of colour'. Firstly colour is lost at the edge of the glass, turning orange/brown and eventually becomes watery white. Over time the colour pigments disintegrate working from the rim towards the centre of the glass.

smell

It is the nose rather than the tongue that gives us the most information when tasting wine. It is said that eighty percent of our sense of taste is from our nose.

We describe a wine's smell as its 'nose' or 'aroma', traditionally described as its 'bouquet'.

WHAT TO DO

SWIRL THE WINE IN THE GLASS By increasing the wine's surface area and its exposure to the air you enable the wine to evolve, or 'open out' in the glass.

TIP THE GLASS Tip it slightly towards you. Again this will increase the surface area of the wine.

TAKE A SHORT SHARP SNIFF Your nose easily becomes used to smells and you want to keep your nose at its freshest, so keep the sniff short.

TAKE A FEW MORE SNIFFS This will allow the wine to reveal more to you, but remember that first impressions count the most.

WHAT TO LOOK OUT FOR

CLEANLINESS Does it smell clean or unclean, pleasant or offensive? Deciding if a wine is in good condition or not is the most important reason for smelling a wine. Some wines do smell of substances that you would not at first associate with wine; mature

Riesling smells of petrol, mature Pinot Noir smells of a farmyard! These smells do not indicate faults. Rotten cabbage, old socks, pear drops, vinegar or cardboard however are some of the smells that *can* indicate your wine is faulty. Some examples of wine faults are as follows:

CORKED A 'corked' wine gives off a foul cardboard odour which comes from a tainted cork. This is due to the cork being infected by a substance called trichloroanisole (TCA).

OXIDATION A wine is said to be oxidised when it loses its fresh fruity aromas and goes stale. This happens when wine is exposed to air. This can occur through a faulty cork. The wine will eventually turn into vinegar.

SULPHUR A wine affected by 'sulphur' smells like hard boiled eggs or a recently struck match. It is not permanent and can be dispersed by swirling the wine in the glass. It is caused by the excessive use of sulphur-dioxide in the winemaking process, used primarily to stop oxidisation in white wines.

FLAVOUR Does the wine smell fruity, floral, vegetal or spicy? Surprisingly few wines smell of grapes. Grapes are made of similar chemical compounds to fruits, vegetables and spices so we are reminded of certain flavours when tasting wine. The aromas can give an idea of the grape varieties used to make the wine and the age of the wine. Older wines tend to smell more savoury and spicy and less fruity than younger wines. See opposite for more detail.

FLAVOUR INTENSITY Does the wine have a faint or pronounced smell? Some grape varieties are more 'aromatic' or perfumed than others.
Aromatic grape varieties: White – Riesling, Gewurztraminer, Sauvignon Blanc and Chenin Blanc. Red – Pinot Noir and Cabernet Franc. The intensity of the flavours also gives you an indication of the origin of the wine: the more intense, the more likely it has been grown in a hot climate.

Wines can be compared to a wide range of naturally occurring products. This chart will help you to identify some of the flavours in wine.

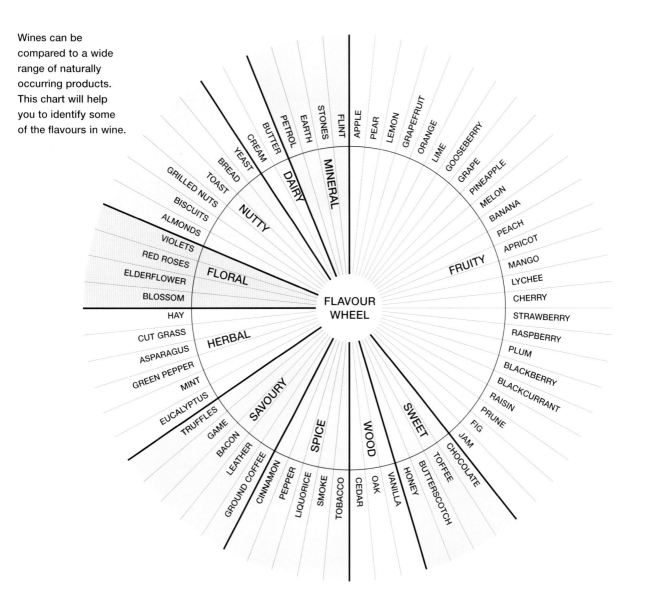

FLAVOUR WHEEL

MINERAL — FLINT, STONES, EARTH, PETROL
DAIRY — BUTTER, CREAM, YEAST
NUTTY — BREAD, TOAST, GRILLED NUTS, BISCUITS, ALMONDS
FLORAL — VIOLETS, RED ROSES, ELDERFLOWER, BLOSSOM
HERBAL — HAY, CUT GRASS, ASPARAGUS, GREEN PEPPER, MINT, EUCALYPTUS
SAVOURY — TRUFFLES, GAME, BACON, LEATHER, GROUND COFFEE
SPICE — CINNAMON, PEPPER, LIQUORICE, SMOKE, TOBACCO
WOOD — CEDAR, OAK, VANILLA, HONEY
SWEET — BUTTERSCOTCH, TOFFEE, CHOCOLATE, JAM, FIG, PRUNE, RAISIN
FRUITY — APPLE, PEAR, LEMON, GRAPEFRUIT, ORANGE, LIME, GOOSEBERRY, GRAPE, PINEAPPLE, MELON, BANANA, PEACH, APRICOT, MANGO, LYCHEE, CHERRY, STRAWBERRY, RASPBERRY, PLUM, BLACKBERRY, BLACKCURRANT

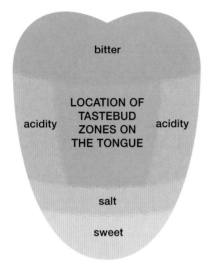

bitter

acidity   **LOCATION OF
TASTEBUD
ZONES ON
THE TONGUE**   acidity

salt

sweet

Certain areas of
the tongue are
sensitive to particular
sensations such as
acidity or sweetness.

taste

Using the sense of taste is more difficult than using the senses
of sight or smell as the wine is in your mouth for a short period only.
Most tastebuds are located in zones on the tongue which are
sensitive to a particular sensation such as sweetness or acidity.
The sense of taste provides the final pieces of the jigsaw and
enables us to draw some conclusions about the wine's quality,
maturity and most importantly whether we like it or not.

WHAT TO DO
SWIRL A MOUTHFUL OF WINE AROUND IN YOUR MOUTH
This enables every tastebud on your tongue to come into
contact with the wine. Hold it in your mouth for a few seconds
to make sure this happens. Professional tasters draw in air at
the same time to increase the wine's contact with air and to
give it a chance to open out on the 'palate'.
SPIT THE WINE OUT INTO A JUG This is optional and depends
on the format of the tasting and how many wines you are tasting.
You can practice doing this over a sink.

WHAT TO LOOK OUT FOR
When tasting wine we look at the different elements which make
up the wine's overall taste. The primary taste elements of sweetness,
acidity, tannin and alcohol provide the wine's structure. The
body and texture of a wine, or the 'mouthfeel', provides us with
an additional dimension to the wine. Its character comes mainly

from its flavours and their intensity. The overall balance of the wine and its 'length' helps us to draw conclusions.

PRIMARY TASTE

SWEETNESS Is the wine dry, medium or sweet? Sweetness is tasted at the tip of the tongue and is associated with white rather than red wines, as most reds are fermented to dryness. Any 'sweetness' in dry reds comes from sweet fruit flavours.

The wine's sweetness comes mainly from the sugar in ripe grapes left after fermentation has finished. This can be controlled by the winemaker.

Sugar in the grapes can be concentrated by harvesting the grapes later than usual. This is known as 'late-harvested' or *'vendange tardive'*. Sometimes, under special climatic conditions, grape skins are affected by 'noble rot' or *'botrytis cinerea'*. This super-concentrates the juice and gives a distinctive honeyed flavour to the wine.

Associated words for sweetness: Ripeness, medium-sweet, intensely sweet, cloying.

Sweet wine grape varieties: All white – Furmint (produces Tokaji in Hungary), Chenin Blanc (produces Demi-Sec or Moelleux Vouvray from the Loire, France), Muscat, Riesling, Semillon and Sauvignon blend (produces Sauternes in Bordeaux, France).

Associated words for dryness: Off-dry, dry, bone-dry.

Dry wine grape varieties: White – Mélon de Bourgogne (produces Muscadet from the Loire, France), Sauvignon

when a red
wine is
ready for
drinking it
should taste
smooth

Blanc (produces Sancerre and Pouilly Fumé from the Loire, France), Chardonnay (produces Chablis from France), Chenin Blanc (produces Savennières and Vouvray Sec from the Loire, France).

ACIDITY Does the wine have a low, medium or high level of acidity? Acidity is tasted on the sides of the tongue and tastes sour like lemons, which makes you salivate.

Acidity occurs naturally in grapes and is important in wines to balance any sweetness. White wines have more natural acidity than red wines.

The riper the fruit becomes, the higher the sugar levels and the lower the acidity levels. Wines produced in cooler climates tend to have higher acidity levels. Cooler countries tend to try to minimise the acidity and maximise ripeness, whereas in hotter climates acidity levels are maximised to balance the ripe fruit levels.

Associated words for high acidity: Refreshing, lively, mouth-watering, crisp, tart.

High acidity grape varieties: White – Sauvignon Blanc, Riesling and Chenin Blanc. Red – Cabernet Franc, Pinot Noir, Sangiovese, Nebbiolo and Gamay.

Low acidity grape varieties: White – Semillon, Viognier, Marsanne and Gewurztraminer.
Red – Cabernet Sauvignon, Merlot and Syrah.

Associated words for lack of acidity: Bland, fat, flabby, cloying (for sweet wines).

TANNIN Does the wine have a low, medium or high level of tannin? Tannin can be tasted at the back of the tongue and on the sides of the mouth. It is bitter and tastes like a strong cup of tea that makes your mouth fur up.

Tannin comes from the skins of the grapes and is found mainly in red wines as they are made using the skins. The thicker the skins of a grape variety, the higher the levels of tannin will be. It is useful as it helps preserve wines and helps them to age. Tannin can also come from oak barrels if they are used in the wine's production. New and smaller barrels 'leach' more tannin into the wine.

When a red wine is ready for drinking, the tannins should be 'integrated' with the other elements in the wine and the wine should taste smooth.

Associated words for high levels of tannin or 'unintegrated' tannins: Harsh, hard, marked, aggressive, astringent.

High tannin grape varieties: All red – Cabernet Sauvignon, Syrah, Nebbiolo, and Sangiovese.

Associated words for low tannin or 'integrated' tannins: Mellow, 'soft', well-integrated, supple.

Low tannin grape varieties: All red – Pinot Noir, Gamay and Cabernet Franc.

ALCOHOL Is the level of alcohol low, medium or high? Alcohol is tasted at the back of the throat and is indicated by a warming sensation.

Hotter countries tend to produce wines that are higher in alcohol. Riper grapes have more sugar which turns into higher levels of alcohol through fermentation. Wines can vary in alcohol from around 8% in German whites to 14.5% or above for red and white wines produced in hot countries such as Australia and California. Wines such as port or sherry which are fortified with spirit have higher alcohol levels.

Associated words for high levels of alcohol: Fierce, fiery.

High alcohol grape varieties: White – Chardonnay, Semillon, Chenin Blanc,

Viognier, Marsanne and Gewurztraminer. Red - Cabernet Sauvignon, Nebbiolo, Sangiovese, Syrah, Grenache and Zinfandel.

Associated words for low levels of alcohol: Watery, lacks 'backbone'.

Low alcohol grape varieties: White - Riesling and Muscat.
Red - Cabernet Franc and Gamay.

BODY Is the wine light, medium or full-bodied - does it feel heavy or light and watery in the mouth? The term body refers to the weight and fullness of the wine in the mouth which gives a thickness to the taste. The body of the wine is defined by the alcohol level and concentration of fruit 'extract'.

Full-bodied grape varieties: White - Chardonnay, Semillon, Viognier, Marsanne and Gewurztraminer. Red - Cabernet Sauvignon, Syrah, Zinfandel and Nebbiolo.

Light-bodied grape varieties: White - Riesling, Sauvignon Blanc, Chenin Blanc (when young) and Mélon de Bourgogne (produces Muscadet from the Loire, France). Red - Gamay, Dolcetto, Cabernet Franc, Pinot Noir, Barbera.

TEXTURE What does the wine feel like in your mouth - does it feel 'smooth' or coarse? The 'texture' of a wine refers to its tactile qualities, and is often compared to fabrics, such as silk.

The texture of a wine is affected by many factors: the degree of alcohol, the level of tannin, the concentration of fruit and, most importantly, the balance of all of the wine's components together.

Associated words for textural qualities: Smooth, soft, velvety, silky, creamy, rich, opulent, mellow, oily and waxy.

Grape varieties with textural qualities: White - Chardonnay, Gewurztraminer, Chenin Blanc (aged and sweet), Semillon.
Red - Pinot Noir, Tempranillo, Nebbiolo, Cabernet Sauvignon and Syrah.

Associated words for lacking texture: Rough, grainy, watery, dilute.

CHARACTER

FLAVOUR What does the wine taste of? Are the flavours reminiscent of any fruits, flowers, spices or herbs?

The flavours found in wines mostly come from the grape varieties used to make them. These flavours are similar to those found when smelling wines. Most grape varieties have distinctive aromas and tastes. Older red wines tend to taste more savoury and spicy, whilst older white wines tend to taste more honeyed. Younger wines tend to taste of fruit.

Associated words: See pages 33 and 48-55.

FLAVOUR INTENSITY Are the flavours weak or pronounced? This refers to the degree of the 'concentration' of flavours in the wine.

Associated words for pronounced flavours: Concentrated, intense.

Grape varieties which can produce pronounced flavours: White - Sauvignon Blanc, Riesling, Muscat, Gewurztraminer, Viognier and Chenin Blanc (when aged and sweet). Red - Cabernet Sauvignon, Cabernet Franc, Tempranillo and Syrah.

Associated words for weak flavours: Dilute, watery, dull.

CONCLUSIONS

BALANCE Is the wine well balanced or unbalanced? Balance refers to whether or not all of the wine's components have come together in harmony and are blended into a whole. The elements in an unbalanced wine remain separate and discernable.

Every wine should achieve a level of balance by the time it is ready to drink. Some fine wines take time to mature before reaching this stage. Balance is a mark of quality, not necessarily price.

LENGTH Is the length short, medium or long? How long does the taste of the wine linger in your mouth after you have swallowed it or spat it out? Generally, the longer the length, the higher the quality of the wine.

tasting notes
can provide a
useful record
for the future

TASTING CONCLUSIONS

Now we have pieced together the story by listening to what each of the senses has to say, we can draw some conclusions. The most important is whether or not you like the wine.

QUALITY Assessing the quality of the wine is probably one of the most important conclusions. A wine's quality is defined by its balance or its potential to become balanced after ageing, its complexity and its length.

A 'complex' wine possesses a variety of flavours, often found in layers. Subtlety is often part of this where flavours are delicate rather than overpowering. We also refer to this as 'finesse'.

Try to assess if the wine has come up to your expectations with regards to price, classification, producer or vintage.

MATURITY Deciding if the wine is ready to drink, or how long it will be until it is ready, is another important reason for tasting. Fine wine benefits from ageing in oak barrel and in bottle. The wine becomes smoother, less fruity and develops a more complex spectrum of flavours. Exactly when each wine is at its optimal point for drinking is difficult to judge. Many factors affect the timing: vintage, grape variety, region, producer and the conditions under which the wine has been kept after bottling. Tasting at regular intervals is a good way of keeping track of a wine's development.

TASTING NOTES Writing wine tasting notes involves describing something sensuous with words, which can be difficult. Remember to use words that mean something to you.

Composing tasting notes can provide a useful personal record to refer back to in the future. They can help to log in your mind the sensations you experience. Including a score or rating can provide a quick reference to show which wine you preferred.

The Tasting Notes template (page 46) is a useful starting point for creating your own tasting notes. Photocopy and use this template as a guide to what to look for when tasting wine. Firstly fill in the wine's full details including producer and vintage. Without this information, tasting notes are worthless. As you taste the wine you can either circle the appropriate words or add your own. Finally try to describe your overall impression of the wine, drawing on its key features. For example - 'Light red in colour with pronounced almond and cherry aromas. This wine shows rich jammy raspberry fruit on the palate, with soft tannins and a lingering finish'.

TASTING NOTES

NAME OF WINE (including vintage, producer, region etc)

Where Purchased:

When Purchased:

Retail Price:

SENSES – WHAT TO LOOK FOR	WORDS TO USE – WHICH OF THE FOLLOWING ARE RELEVANT?	COMMENTS ON KEY FEATURES
SIGHT		
Clarity	clear, dull	
Bubbles	fizzy, still	
Thickness	oily, watery	
Deposits	present, absent	
Colour: White	lemon, gold	
Colour: Red	purple, crimson, red-brown	
Colour: Rosé	orange, pink	
Depth of Colour	pale, intense (at rim and core)	
SMELL		
Cleanliness	clean, unclean	
Flavour	fruity, floral, vegetal, spicy	
Flavour Intensity	weak, pronounced	
TASTE		
Sweetness	dry, medium, sweet	
Acidity	low, medium, high	
Tannin	low, medium, high	
Alcohol	low, medium, high	
Flavour	fruity, floral, vegetal, spicy	
Flavour Intensity	faint, pronounced	
Balance	good, unbalanced	
Length	short, medium, long	

Body	light, medium, full
Texture	smooth, coarse

CONCLUSIONS

Quality	poor, acceptable, good
Maturity	immature, ready to drink, over the hill

OVERALL ASSESSMENT

SCORE your overall impression of the wine out of 20

Photocopy this template to use at
your own wine tastings. Remember,
use words that mean something to you
and this form will be a useful reference.

key grape varieties

CHARDONNAY

KEY FLAVOURS Melon, nuts, butter, pineapple, apple, vanilla (if aged in oak).

IDENTITY Adaptable, high in alcohol, no pronounced characteristics of its own so responds to its environment, moderate to high acidity, likes oak, best young except Burgundy.

KEY REGIONS Burgundy in France, Champagne in France (blended with Pinot Noir and Pinot Meunier), Australia, California, South Africa, New Zealand.

SAUVIGNON BLANC

KEY FLAVOURS Asparagus, gooseberry, grassy.

IDENTITY Aromatic, high acidity, often blended with Semillon to produce dry and sweet styles, does not like oak unless blended, age only when blended.

KEY REGIONS The Loire (Pouilly-Fumé and Sancerre) and Bordeaux in France (Péssac-Leognan when blended), New Zealand, Chile, California, Australia.

SEMILLON

KEY FLAVOURS Fig, lime, cut grass, lemon, nectarine (dry). Wax, honey, orange, toast (sweet).

IDENTITY Heavy body, waxy texture, low acidity, high alcohol, often blended with Sauvignon Blanc to produce dry and sweet styles, does not like oak unless blended, age when blended, affected by noble rot.

KEY REGIONS Dry – Bordeaux in France (Péssac-Leognan when blended). Australia (Hunter Valley, Barossa Valley, Western Australia). Sweet – Bordeaux (Sauternes and Barsac, blended with Sauvignon Blanc), Australia.

CHENIN BLANC

KEY FLAVOURS Almond, lemon, apple, damp straw, flowers (dry). Honey, wet wool, spice, beeswax (sweet)

IDENTITY High in acidity, does not like oak, high alcohol, pungent, wide range of styles, age sweeter styles and dry powerful styles.

KEY REGIONS Dry – The Loire in France, South Africa. Sweet – The Loire (Vouvray, Coteaux du Layon).

RIESLING

KEY FLAVOURS Rhubarb, floral, mineral, green apple, lime. Petrol, honey (with age).

IDENTITY Low to medium alcohol, high acidity, does not like oak (particularly new oak), dry and late-harvested sweet styles, affected by noble rot, aromatic.

KEY REGIONS Germany (Mosel, Pfalz, Nahe, Rheingau, Rheinhessen), Austria, Alsace in France, Australia, New Zealand, USA.

GEWURZTRAMINER

KEY FLAVOURS Lychees, turkish delight, rose petals.

IDENTITY Very distinctive acquired taste, aromatic, low acidity and high alcohol gives an oily texture, does not like oak, age only sweet styles, sweet wines are late-harvested, drink young.

KEY REGIONS Alsace in France.

VIOGNIER

KEY FLAVOURS Peaches, apricot, nutmeg, cream.

IDENTITY High in alcohol, low in acidity, rich texture, best enjoyed young, distinctive aromatic qualities.

KEY REGIONS Northern Rhône in France (Condrieu), Languedoc-Roussillon in France, California, Australia, South America.

MARSANNE

KEY FLAVOURS Marzipan, almond.

IDENTITY High in alcohol, low in acid, often blended with Roussanne, heaviness of texture on the palate.

KEY REGIONS Northern Rhône in France (Hermitage), Southern France, Australia, California.

MUSCAT

KEY FLAVOURS Grape, orange blossom.

IDENTITY Wide range of styles mostly medium-sweet to sweet, light and naturally low in alcohol, can be fortified.

KEY REGIONS Rhône in France (particularly Clairette de Die and sweet Vin Doux Naturel), Southern France, Northern Italy (particularly Moscato d'Asti and Asti Spumante), Australia (particularly Liqueur Muscat from Rutherglen, Victoria), California, South Africa.

CABERNET-SAUVIGNON

KEY FLAVOURS Blackcurrant, mint, chocolate, tobacco, cedar wood, cigar box.

IDENTITY Versatile, deep colour, high level of tannin, good ageing potential, influenced by oak, best when blended with Merlot and Cabernet Franc.

KEY REGIONS Bordeaux in France (particularly in the Médoc when blended), Australia, Chile, USA.

PINOT NOIR

KEY FLAVOURS Violets, cherry, aroma of a farmyard (with age), earthy.

IDENTITY Rich silky texture, most successful as a varietal, blended in Champagne, influenced by oak, good ageing potential, thin-skinned so light in colour, delicate and low in tannin, high in acidity.

KEY REGIONS Burgundy in France, Champagne in France (blended with Chardonnay and Pinot Meunier). New Zealand (Martinborough), USA (Oregon and Carneros, California), Australia (particularly Victoria and Tasmania).

SYRAH/SHIRAZ

KEY FLAVOURS Black pepper, redcurrant, blackberry, tobacco, smoke, burnt rubber.

IDENTITY High alcohol, high in tannin, moderate acidity, takes well to new oak, varietal and blended, good ageing qualities.

KEY REGIONS Northern Rhône in France (Côte Rôtie and Hermitage), Southern Rhône in France (particularly Châteauneuf-du-Pape, when blended), Australia (Barossa Valley, Hunter Valléy and McLaren Vale), USA (California and Washington State).

MERLOT

KEY FLAVOURS Coffee, ripe plums, fruitcake, black pepper.

IDENTITY Low in acidity, soft in texture with low tannin levels, juicy, usually blended with Cabernet Sauvignon and Cabernet Franc, influenced by oak, good ageing for quality wines.

KEY REGIONS Bordeaux in France (particularly St Emilion and Pomerol when blended), Chile, USA (Washington State, California), Argentina, South Africa, Australia.

CABERNET FRANC

KEY FLAVOURS Pencil shavings, raspberry, tobacco, grass.

IDENTITY Pale in colour, low in tannin, aromatic, high in acidity, light in body, early drinking as a varietal, fine texture.

KEY REGIONS Bordeaux in France (blended with Cabernet Sauvignon and Merlot), the Loire in France (particularly Chinon, St Nicolas de Bourgeuil, Saumur Champigny), South America.

GRENACHE

KEY FLAVOURS Liquorice, raspberry, smoke, herbs.

IDENTITY Usually blended, high alcohol, range of styles from light to powerful wines, low acidity.

KEY REGIONS Southern Rhône in France (Châteauneuf-du-Pape, Vacqueyras, Gigondas, Côtes du Rhône), Southern France, Spain, Australia.

GAMAY

KEY FLAVOURS Strawberry, bubble gum, banana.

IDENTITY High in acidity, low in tannin, early drinking, does not like oak, usually a varietal.

KEY REGIONS Beaujolais in France (particularly the ten Beaujolais *Crus*) and the Loire in France.

SANGIOVESE
KEY FLAVOURS Cold tea, herbs, black cherry.
IDENTITY Moderate colour, medium-bodied, high tannin and acidity, often blended, develops an orange rim with age.
KEY REGIONS Italy (particularly Brunello di Montalcino, Chianti), South America.

TEMPRANILLO
KEY FLAVOURS Vanilla, strawberry, tobacco.
IDENTITY Moderate acidity and tannin, usually part of a blend, smooth and sweet scented, likes American oak.
KEY REGIONS Spain (particularly Rioja, Ribera del Duero, Navarra and Valdepenas), South America.

ZINFANDEL
KEY FLAVOURS Blueberry, blackberry, mixed spices.
IDENTITY Juiciness, high in alcohol, gets very ripe, high concentration of fruit, dark colour.
KEY REGIONS California (particularly Sonoma), Southern Italy (known as Primitivo).

NEBBIOLO
KEY FLAVOURS Prunes, roses, truffle, leather, tar (with age).
IDENTITY High acidity, tannin and alcohol, likes new oak, powerful, moderate colour.
KEY REGIONS Piedmont in Northern Italy (particularly Barolo and Barbaresco).

food and wine matching

Enjoying wine and food together is one of life's greatest pleasures, particularly when shared with friends and family. Matching the right wines with the food on your plate, however, can seem challenging.

Reassuringly most wines can be enjoyed with most foods. There are no rights and wrongs. It is a matter of personal taste. Do not be daunted by the huge variety of wines now available. Use this range to your advantage. Above all have fun and do not be afraid to experiment. You may come across a combination which is 'made in heaven'. When this happens, this can be a truly unforgettable experience.

FORGET THE COLOUR OF WINES

Matching food and wine is more to do with the strength of flavour of the wines rather than their colour.

Red wine has often been matched with cheese but this is far from the perfect match it is made out to be. Rather than red wines, it is medium-dry whites which often complement cheeses. Many cheeses have a mouth-coating texture which clashes with most red wines. If you prefer red, then choose a wine with a low level of tannin with this type of cheese. Full-bodied red wines are best with hard cheeses with strong flavours.

White wines are said to be best matched with fish. It is the iodine in the fish and the tannin in red wines that can make the fish taste metallic. Either choose a white wine or, if you prefer red, choose an example with a low level of tannin – from the Pinot Noir, Gamay or the Barbera grape varieties for example.

MATCH STRENGTHS OF FLAVOURS

When matching wine with food, try to think of the weight and strength of the

flavour of the food. Choose a wine that is similar in strength. It is easiest to think of wine as a sauce that you are adding to the food. The stronger the flavour, the bigger or more full-bodied the wine needs to be. Or keep the wine simple and let the food dominate, and vice versa.

Sometimes a dish has dominant types of flavours such as sweetness and acidity that need addressing. You can either complement or contrast these flavours with the wine you choose.

RICHNESS Acidity in the wine provides an excellent foil to richness in food.

ACIDITY Choose a wine with acidity levels equal to that in the food.

SWEETNESS Choose a wine with an equal or more pronounced levels of sweetness.

SALTINESS Contrast salty food with sweet wine, for example port and salty Stilton.

white wine
styles

FRESH AND DRY
EXAMPLES OF GRAPE VARIETIES Young Chenin Blanc (e.g. from South Africa), Sauvignon Blanc (e.g. Sancerre, Pouilly Fumé from the Loire, France), Chardonnay (e.g. unoaked Chablis from France), Melon de Bourgogne (e.g. Muscadet from the Loire, France).
IDEAL WITH Salads, delicately flavoured fish, seafood pasta, oysters (particularly well-matched to Chablis), seafood (particularly well-matched to Muscadet), chicken dishes, goats' cheese.

AROMATIC MEDIUM DRY
EXAMPLES OF GRAPE VARIETIES Riesling, Muscat, Viognier, Gewurztraminer, Tokay Pinot Gris, Chenin Blanc (e.g. Vouvray from the Loire in France).
IDEAL WITH Spicy Eastern flavours, foie gras (particularly well-matched to Tokay Pinot Gris), soft cheeses like Camembert or Brie.

RICH AND FULL-BODIED

EXAMPLES OF GRAPE VARIETIES Chardonnay (e.g. from the New World and Burgundy from France), Viognier (e.g. Condrieu, from the Northern Rhône, France), Marsanne and Roussanne blend (e.g. Hermitage from the Northern Rhône, France), Semillon (e.g. from Australia).

IDEAL WITH Fish such as turbot, lobster (particularly well-matched to New World Chardonnays), oily fish such as mackerel and sardines, smoked salmon, crab, prawns, scallops, poultry particularly in sauces, pork and veal, creamy pasta.

SWEET WINES

EXAMPLES OF GRAPE VARIETIES Medium-sweet: Muscat (e.g. Asti Spumante and Moscato from Piedmont, Italy), Riesling (e.g. Auslese and Beerenauslese from Germany and *vendange tardive* from Alsace, France), Chenin Blanc (*moelleux* e.g. Coteaux du Layon from the Loire, France).

Sweet: Muscat (e.g. Vin Doux Naturel from the Rhône, France and sweet Muscat from California), Riesling (e.g. Trockenbeerenauslese from Germany), Furmint (e.g. Tokaji from Hungary), Gewurztraminer (e.g. *vendange tardive* from Alsace, France), Semillon and Sauvignon Blanc blend (e.g. Sauternes or Barsac from Bordeaux, France).

Very Sweet: Muscat (e.g. Australian Liqueur from Rutherglen, Victoria).

IDEAL WITH Desserts, foie gras, blue cheese.

rosé wine styles

EXAMPLES OF GRAPE VARIETIES Cabernet Franc (e.g. Rosé d'Anjou from the Loire, France), Pinot Noir (e.g. Sancerre Rosé from the Loire, France), Grenache and Cinsault blend (e.g. Tavel Rosé from the Southern Rhône), Mourvèdre (e.g. Provence Rosé from South of France).

IDEAL WITH Pasta, pizza, fish, cold meats, ham, salami, patés, summer picnics and barbecues.

RAMS

Lot #12 1998
CALIFORNIA
PINOT NOIR

CELLARED & BOTTLED BY C. BR...
OAKVILLE, CALIFOR...
...COHOL 13% BY VOL...

red wine
styles

LIGHT AND FRUITY
EXAMPLES OF GRAPE VARIETIES Gamay
(e.g. Beaujolais in France), Pinot Noir (e.g. Burgundy
in France and Sancerre Rouge in the Loire, France),
Tempranillo (e.g. unoaked Rioja, Ribera del Duero),
Dolcetto (e.g. Dolcetto from Piedmont, Italy),
Cabernet Franc (e.g. Chinon and St Nicholas de
Bourgueil in the Loire, France).
IDEAL WITH Pasta, pizza, fish, cold meats, ham,
salami, patés, summer picnics and barbecues.

SMOOTH, MEDIUM-BODIED
EXAMPLES OF GRAPE VARIETIES Tempranillo
(e.g. oaked Rioja in Spain), Syrah (e.g. Crozes
Hermitage from the Northern Rhône, France),
Cabernet Sauvignon (e.g. South of France), Merlot
(e.g. from the New World and the South of France),
Pinot Noir (e.g. Burgundy in France and from the
New World), Sangiovese (e.g. Chianti from Tuscany,
Italy), blend of Grenache and Syrah (e.g. Côtes du
Rhône from France), blend of Cabernet Sauvignon
and Merlot (e.g. Bordeaux, France).

IDEAL WITH Mild flavoured game (pheasant,
boar, rabbit, quail, duck), Camembert cheese
(particularly well-matched to Pinot Noir), pork,
veal, poultry, red meats, meat casseroles.

FULL-BODIED
EXAMPLES OF GRAPE VARIETIES Syrah/Shiraz (e.g.
Cornas, Côte Rôtie or Hermitage from
the Nothern Rhône in France), Cabernet
Sauvignon (e.g. from the New World), Nebbiolo
(e.g. Barolo from Piedmont, Italy), Zinfandel
(e.g. from California), Grenache and Syrah
blend (e.g. Châteauneuf-du-Pape from the
Southern Rhône, France), Cabernet Sauvignon
and Merlot blend (e.g. in the New World),
Shiraz and Cabernet Sauvignon blend (e.g. from
the New World).
IDEAL WITH Stronger flavoured game (hare,
venison, pigeon), red meats such as beef and lamb,
hard strong flavoured cheeses.

glossary

ACIDITY The sharpness in wines.

AERATING Bringing the wine into contact with air to accelerate its development.

ALCOHOL Sugar in ripe grapes turns into alcohol to produce wine.

AROMA Smell of a wine.

AROMATIC Perfumed grape varieties.

BACKBONE Structure of a wine.

BALANCE The integration of acid, tannin, alcohol, fruit and flavour in wine.

BLEND Mixture of grape varieties.

BODY Weight and fullness of a wine on the palate.

BOTRYTIS CINEREA 'Noble rot' – results in super concentration and sweetness.

BOUQUET The smell of a wine.

BREAKING UP Colour pigments disintegrate in old red wines.

BREATH Leaving wine in contact with air to open out.

COMPLEXITY Wines possessing a variety of flavours.

CONCENTRATION Depth, richness and intensity of fruit in a wine.

CORE Colour of wine in the centre of a glass.

CORKED Wine fault – musty odour.

DECANTING Pouring the wine out of the bottle into a decanter or jug.

EXTRACT Concentration of fruit in a wine.

FERMENTATION Process whereby sugar in the juice of ripe grapes turns into alcohol to produce wine.

FINE WINE A superior quality wine which generally benefits from ageing.

FINESSE Complexity and subtlety in wine.

FLAVOUR Aroma and taste of a wine compared to fruits, spices etc.

FORTIFIED Wine strengthened by the addition of alcohol.

FULL-BODIED Wines with a high level of fruit concentration and alcohol.

INTEGRATED Tannins in a wine that are harmonious with the other components.

INTENSITY The depth and richness of flavour in a wine.

LEACH Tannins in oak barrel soaking into wine.

LEGS Oily texture left on the inside of the glass by some wines.

LENGTH How long the taste of wine lasts in the mouth after tasting.

MOUTHFEEL How the wine feels in the mouth, its texture, weight and body.

NEW WORLD 'Newer' wine producing countries (Australia, South Africa, South America, USA, New Zealand).

NOSE Smell of a wine.

OAKED Wine aged in oak barrels.

OLD WORLD 'Older' wine producing countries – Europe.

OXIDISED Wine that has lost its freshness as a result of over exposure to air.

PALATE The taste of a wine in the mouth.

RICH Good concentration of ripe fruit.

SOFT Wine that is rounded, fruity and low in tannin.

SMOOTH Wine with good fruit levels and soft integrated tannins.

SPARKLING Wine with bubbles.

SPRITZ A slight sparkle in a wine.

STYLE The type of wine produced.

SULPHUR Pungent smell which can be dispersed by swirling the glass.

SWEETNESS Unfermented sugar in the wine from the ripeness of the grapes.

TANNIN A dry bitterness in wine.

TARTRATES Harmless crystals that can be found in both red and white wines.

TEARS Oily texture left on the inside of the glass by some wines.

TERROIR Effect of soil, grape variety, climate and aspect on a wine's taste.

TEXTURE What the wine feels like in the mouth, often compared to fabrics.

VARIETAL Wines made from a single dominant grape variety.

VENDAGE TARDIVE Late-harvesting which produces sweetness.

VISCOSITY Thickness in a wine with a great density of fruit extract and alcohol indicated by 'tears' and 'legs'.

index

acidity, 8, 34, 37, 57
age of vines, 10
age of wine, colour and, 29
ageing wine, 13, 45
alcohol, 8
  body, 41
  levels of, 38–41
  taste, 34
  viscosity, 26
Alsace, 8
aroma, 30–2
Australia, 8, 10, 12

balance, 43
Barbera, 38, 41, 56
blended wines, 8–10
blind tasting, 17–19
body, 34, 41
Bordeaux, 10
botrytis cinerea, 36
bottles, 17–19, 18
bouquet, 30
'breaking up of colour', 29
bubbles, 24

Cabernet Franc, 10, 32, 37, 38, 41, 43, 54, 59, 61
Cabernet Sauvignon, 10, 13, 26, 37, 38, 41, 43, 52, 61

California, 8, 12
Chablis, 8, 29
Champagne, 10
character, 34–6, 43
Chardonnay, 8, 10, 13, 26, 37, 38, 41, 48, 58, 59
cheese, matching wine to, 56
Chenin Blanc, 13, 26, 32, 36, 37, 38, 41, 43, 49, 58, 59
Cinsault, 59
clarity, 24
classification systems, 10–12
cleanliness, 30–2
climate, 10, 12, 29, 37
colour, 26–9, 27–9
complex wines, 45
corked wine, 32
corks, 26
corkscrews, 15
Corvina, 61

decanting, 19
deposits, 26, 26
depth of colour, 29
Dolcetto, 41, 61
dry wines, 36–7, 58

fine wines, 13
finesse, 45
fish, matching wine to, 56
flavour intensity, 32, 43
flavours, 32, 33, 43, 56–7

foil-cutters, 15
food, matching wine to, 56–61
formal tastings, 17
fortified wines, 8
France, 8, 10
full-bodied wines, 41, 59, 61
Furmint, 36, 59

Gamay, 37, 38, 41, 54, 56, 61
Germany, 8, 10–12
Gewurztraminer, 26, 32, 37, 41, 43, 50, 58, 59
glasses, 14, 15, 24
grape varieties, 8–10, 26
  acidity, 37
  ageing wine, 13
  alcohol content, 38–41
  aromatic grapes, 32
  body, 41
  dry wines, 36–7
  flavour intensity, 32, 43
  flavours, 43
  rosé wines, 59
  sweet wines, 59
  sweetness, 36
  tannin, 38
  texture, 41
  wine styles, 58–61
Grenache, 54, 59, 61

informal tastings, 17
Italy, 12

labels, 11, 12
late-harvested grapes, 36
length, 36, 43
light-bodied wines, 41, 61

madeira, 8
Marsanne, 37, 41, 51, 59
maturity, 45
Melon de Bourgogne, 36, 41, 58
Merlot, 10, 13, 37, 53, 61
Mosel, 29
Mourvèdre, 59
mouthfeel, 34
Muscat, 36, 41, 43, 51, 58, 59

Nebbiolo, 13, 37, 38, 41, 55, 61
New World wines, 10, 12
New Zealand, 10
noble-rot, 36
North America, 10
nose, 10, 30–2

oak barrels, ageing wine, 13, 38, 45
Old World wines, 10, 12
opening wines, 19
oxidation, 20, 29, 32

palate, 10, 34
Pinot Gris, 58

Pinot Meunier, 10
Pinot Noir, 10, 13, 26, 32, 37, 38, 41, 52, 56, 59, 61
port, 8

quality, 45

red wines
  ageing, 13
  alcohol content, 38
  colour, 26, 28, 29
  flavours, 43
  matching food to, 56
  serving temperature, 20
  styles, 61
  tannin, 38
regions, 10–12
richness, matching food to wine, 57
Riesling, 13, 26, 30–2, 36, 37, 41, 43, 50, 58, 59
rosé wines
  colour, 29

grape varieties, 59
  serving temperature, 20
Roussanne, 59

saltiness, matching food to wine, 57
Sangiovese, 13, 26, 37, 38, 41, 55, 61
Sauvignon Blanc, 26, 32, 36–7, 41, 43, 48, 58, 59
sediment, 26
Semillon, 13, 36, 37, 38, 41, 49, 59
sherry, 8
Shiraz see Syrah
sight, 24–9
smell, 30–3
South Africa, 10, 12
South America, 10
Spain, 10
sparkling wines, 8
spittoons, 15
styles of wine, 8, 58–61

sugar
  alcohol content, 38
  sweetness, 36
sulphur, 32
sweetness, 8, 34, 36, 57, 59
Syrah/Shiraz, 13, 26, 37, 38, 41, 43, 53, 61

tannin, 8, 20, 34, 38, 56
tartrates, 26, 26
taste, 34–43
tastebuds, 34
tasting notes, 17, 45, 46–7
temperature, serving wine, 19–20
template, tasting notes, 45, 46–7
Tempranillo, 41, 43, 55, 61
terroir, 10–12
texture, 24–6, 34, 41
Tokay, 58
tongue, tastebuds, 34
trichloroanisole (TCA), 32

varietal wines, 8
vendange tardive, 36
vinegar, 32
vines, age, 10
vintages, 8, 12
Viognier, 26, 37, 41, 43, 51, 58, 59
viscosity, 26

white wines
  ageing, 13
  alcohol content, 38
  colour, 26, 27, 29
  flavours, 43
  matching food to, 56
  serving temperature, 20
  styles, 58–9
winemakers, 13

Zinfandel, 26, 41, 55, 61

acknowledgments

Thanks to the following; Simon Field, Mandy Woodard, Gail Barnett for their time and advice, Simon Berry of wine merchants Berry Bros. & Rudd for standing by me and Nick Croft for his continual support.

Berry Bros. & Rudd
3 St James's Street
London SW1A 1EG
www.bbr.com